THE CAELi Review

VOLUME 1 No. 3 | May 2024

LETTER FROM THE EDITOR
HAWK GRUBB
    How Many Ways Does a Crossroad Make?   PAGE 5

PALLAS K AUGUSTINE
    Abandoning the Night:
    Technology, Optimization, and
    Recovering a Relational Astrology   PAGE 6

GIACOMO ALBANO
    "Earthly Stars": The Cycles
    of the Stars in Natal Astrology   PAGE 15

MATT TREASE
    ...from *In the Belly: an Imbolc daysong*   PAGE 25

ROBERT P. BLASCHKE
    Progression Theory   PAGE 27

ALEXANDRA NAGEL
    C. Aq. Libra:
    Roelf Takens (1862–1930),
    Esoteric Astrologer and Writer   PAGE 30

PETER O'LEARY
    ...from *Onlikenesses*   PAGE 49

revelore press

CONTRIBUTORS TO THIS ISSUE:

Alexandra H. M. Nagel is an independent Dutch historian of western esotericism. She obtained her master's in this field in 2007 at the University of Amsterdam and finished her thesis work on the hand-reader Julius Spier (1887–1942) at Leiden University in 2020. ORCID: https://orcid.org/0000-0003-3162-1355; correspondence: xnagel@yahoo.com.

Giacomo Albano is a specialist in stellar astrology, horary and electional astrology and astrological magic based in Italy. Among his latest publications are: *Advanced Stellar Astrology, Mundane Stellar Astrology, Ancient Egypt, Jerusalem and the Stars....* www.astrologiaprevisionale.net

Hawk Grubb is a magician, diarist, and professional astrologer/magical mentor living in the Pacific Northwest. In another life you'd have found them delivering prophecy, bent over the cracks in the cave floor at Pytho. In this life, you can find them doing the same thing, but like, on the computer.

Matt Trease (poet/astrologer) lives on the homeland of the Duwamish people (Tukwila, WA). He serves on the board of the Cascadia Poetics Lab, co-curates the Margin Shift reading series, and is poetry editor for the CAELi Review. His debut poetry collection, The Outside is forthcoming from Carbonation Press in Summer/Fall 2024.

Pallas K. Augustine is a writer, astrologer, educator, and consultant. Their practice is rooted in a relational approach that aims to deeply connect us with our non-human and non-living kin as well as to each other. Their book *The IC: An Astrology of Coming Home* is forthcoming in 2024.

Peter O'Leary is the author of *The Hidden Eyes of Things*, a book-length poem about astrology and the unconscious. He lives in Oak Park, Illinois and teaches at the School of the Art Institute of Chicago. With John Tipton, he edits Verge Books.

Robert P. Blaschke (1953–2011), founder of the Earthwalk School of Astrology, was an internationally celebrated professional astrologer who served as president of the Washington State and Oregon Astrological Associations, as well as a coordinator for the International Society for Astrological Research. In 2012 he won the Marion D. March Regulus Award for Discovery, Innovation and Research. His five-volume "Astrology: A Language of Life" series will be reissued by Revelore Press in 2024.

LETTER FROM THE EDITOR

Salutations to the Readers of the CAELi Review!

I am thrilled to present to you the latest edition of *The CAELi Review*, Volume One, Issue Three. As we welcome the arrival of spring (in the northern hemisphere) and celebrate Beltane, we invite you to indulge in a delightful collection of materials that our contributors have carefully crafted for you all. This issue promises to be a treat for all astrology enthusiasts, with a sparkling blend of thought-provoking articles and poems.

Our third issue comprises three articles, three poems, and an exclusive three-page excerpt from the upcoming republication of Robert P. Blaschke's seminal work, *Progressions*. Revelore Press plans to republish the book in sequence with Blaschke's other volumes in his "Astrology: A Language of Life" series in the coming months. To promote our highly anticipated summer course on Advanced Progressions for Kepler College, we have included a dash of Blaschke's wisdom in this issue.

Jenn Zahrt and I will co-teach the course, which begins this July, demonstrating how to weave different scales and directions of time with clarity. Including tertiary, minor, and converse progressions, we want to help you conceptualize faster time scales, visualize their layering, and apply their overlapping and fractal storylines. We will also apply fixed stars to the picture as an alternative route to Blaschke's use of Sabian Symbols. If you are interested in enhancing your work with progressions and sharpening your notions of symbolic astrological time, we hope that this offering sparks your interest.

Our contributors to this issue have brought forth a rich tapestry of materials that offer diverse and unique perspectives on astrology and its applications. Our articles range from modernizing astrological approaches while staying rooted in ancestral and historical context, exploring the life and work of a prominent figure in the early 20th-century occult and astrological movements, to a deep dive into stellar astrology techniques applied to nativities. These articles are a treasure trove of diverse insights that are sure to pique your interest, broaden your horizons, and challenge your beliefs.

Our poetry selections offer a deeper understanding of the purpose of astrology and its role in helping us navigate life's crossroads. These works of art encourage us to discover hidden unities behind apparent discontinuities, find the true meaning behind the values or curses of approximations, and value lunar discontinuities as rhythmic time.

We hope that this issue enriches your perspectives and inspires you to explore new facets of the fascinating world of astrology. Don't forget to become a member of the CAELi Institute to stay in the loop on our future issues and courses. May the wisdom of the stars ever guide your curiosity.

In gratitude,
Cameron Cassidy
Editor, *The CAELi Review*
Salem, Massachusetts
May 4, 2024

HAWK GRUBB

How many ways does a crossroad make?

five slices of peach on her offering plate.
There *were* six, but one I ate.
she laughed when I placed them at her feet,
And said "one is for you—
Decide which to take."

PALLAS K. AUGUSTINE

Abandoning the Night: Technology, Optimization, and Recovering a Relational Astrology

ASTROLOGERS HAVE ALWAYS BEEN NERDS. The temperament required to track the events and images of the celestial spheres—let alone to make poetry and medicine out of them—often goes hand-in-hand with an openness to technologies that support the sheer scale and ease of tracking that can be accomplished. Whether the technology is carved clay tables of calculation, a medieval astrolabe, a library of cross-cultural texts, a modern digital ephemeris, or advanced 3D visioning software, our profession constantly adapts to the tools and texts we are able to access.

Since the human experience of the practice of astrology is as much a concern as the celestial component for most astrologers, technologies and techniques may be abandoned or adapted again when they begin to threaten connection to embodied and relational realities. In recent years, the churn of sensationalized social media and personalized horoscopic apps have incentivized a relentless and addictive loop of astrological transit play-by-plays. At the same time, these developments have stirred a rise in popular appreciation for astrology as a daily practice. The same technologies that allow us to share previously inconceivable amounts of information—astrological and otherwise—in barely imaginable fractions of time, now overwhelm any semblance of coherent narrative.

Astrology, when understood as a craft and an ancestral practice—as divination, as collaboration between seen and unseen forces, between human and more-than-human—is a narrative technology. In *Vita Comtemplativa: A Praise of Inactivity*, Byung-Chul Han writes, "We are very well informed, yet, in the absence of narrative, we are without orientation."[1] As a narrative technology, astrology is also an orienting device. The circular chart with its horizon line, with its risings, culminatings, and settings marks a moment in a local place *on Earth.* The poetry of lived experience that winds and whirls out of that moment cannot be easily quantified and abstracted. Hyperdigitization and the primacy of information over story devalues the orienting role of astrology as an ancient narrative technology.

Alongside the deluge of disorienting information overload wrought by Neptune in Pisces, the accompanying re-enchantment, rewilding, and reimagining seem to be hitting limits in the technological sphere. With Saturn now co-present, an internet filled with A.I. bots blows algorithms to extremes as humans are left wading through the sewage of stolen and regurgitated "content." With the dignified Saturn years behind us, their themes of lineage, tradition, structural integrity, fault lines, legacy, and vulnerability pervade the critiques brought toward the current maelstrom of technological saturation, critiques that will mature just in time for Saturn-Neptune in Aries. We are in the foreshadowing of the reorientation that Aries will bring.

Many of us, as practitioners, students, producers, and consumers of astrology, are already responding to an over-technologized, hyperdigitalized, solipsistic, atomized astrology. Many astrologers never abandoned the night, the soil, the ancestors, the magic, the dance, the whispering spirits of the chart that continue to grow louder as our voices join theirs, but many have turned away from soul in a quest for scientific materialist validation. In a chapter from the forthcoming *The IC: An Astrology of Coming Home*, I observe how some recent shifts in the astrological industry map onto significant cultural developments: we have seen the rising popularity of an embodied turn toward astrology, toward more visible sky astrology with the proliferation of a recovered seven-planet rulership scheme, as well as a relational turn toward direct spirit contact and astrological magic with the whole animated sky and not just the ecliptic. These developments fulfill a prophecy of Robert Blaschke, as disseminated by CAELi Founder Jenn Zahrt, of the Uranus-North Node conjunctions bringing major shifts in the astrological community. The United Astrology Conference 2018 was themed "Earth and Sky," afterall. Uranus had come to Taurus to foretell the demands and gifts of Necessity as we wandered into the uncertain terrain of our New Age of Air with our species still tethered to this beautiful, ruptured, changing Earth.

Venus' rulership of the Uranus-North Node conjunction in Taurus brings to bear the question of values and how we as astrologers, with our disparate individual practices and also as astrologers practicing in a vast collective field, embody our values in the techniques and language we choose and how we structure our offerings. As a discipline of science and art—without the protections of either—astrology is prone to the pitfalls of both: how science is often co-opted by powerful forces and how art denies they are capable of being co-opted. Astrology can be made into both tool and weapon. An astrological practice enacts the values of the practitioner. Each of us has a choice to be intentional about the values, priorities, and worldview our astrology brings to Earth.

As a vast collective field, it isn't possible to control the flow of astrological influence, no matter how much we may want to protect our beautiful astrology from those who would do her harm or use her for harm. There is always a skeptical social scientist lurking in the corner ready to disprove astrology—and gods forbid one of these days they accidentally figure out how to prove its efficacy. I joke, but sometimes scientific validation feels inevitable. The more *popular* legitimacy that astrology (re)gains in the West, the closer it circles to self-help, self-improvement, and self-optimization practices, with all the ideological baggage of those spheres in tow. While supportive of astrology as a consumer industry, the kind of attention brought to a discipline through pop culture trends under late capitalism is bound to dismay many astrologers—as we've witnessed through the last decade. But popular astrology for the layperson—folk astrology, even—has probably always existed alongside the more arcane, highly literate astrology dependent on access to technology and experience.

As part of this drive toward self-optimization, astrology all across the spectrum tends to fall victim to the idea of the "one best way," a framing offered by French polymath Jacques Ellul and taken up by American Christian theologian Michael Sacasas who writes of the consequence of such an idea: "subsequently living with the unyielding pressure to discover it and the inevitable and perpetual frustration of failing to achieve it."[2] The ill effects of such pressure are visible everywhere, not least of which in the epidemic of loneliness.

Optimization culture is the optimized twin of "grind culture," afterall. Deftly addressed by Tricia Hersey of The Nap Ministry in her *Rest is Resistance: A Manifesto*, "Grind culture has made us all human machines, willing and ready to donate our lives to a capitalist system that thrives by placing profits over people."[3] As Hersey elaborates, "we become grind culture," and our bodies and relationships "become less human and less secure."[4] Whereas Hersey offers a full-scale offramp into collective liberatory rest and all of the deprogramming and evacuation that requires, the optimization culture offered by self-improvement and wellness industries is a doubling down, an instrumental mutation in response to the issues: how do we—in the face of the horror and pressure and struggle—become the *most* human and discover the *one best way*? The "natal promise" of astrology is prime territory for optimization culture to take root.

As it stands, contemporary astrology can firmly qualify as a practice of self-optimisation under a 2023 framework developed by sociologists Daniel Nehring and Anja Röcke.[5] Self-optimization practices "encourage individuals to pursue the optimal imaginable version of their bodies, their mental and emotional constitution, and their conduct of everyday life...thus aim[ing] to improve facets of the self in a constant, potentially open-ended and rational way."[6] Nehring and Röcke argue that self-optimisation has a history related to particularly European and American ideas of progress, morality, and rationalization, and also to Romanticism, New Thought, and humanistic psychology[7]—the latter worlds often cross-pollinated with astrology and occultism.

Astrology's connection with practices that could fall under the self-optimisation umbrella are not new, of course. Various tributaries of astrology, magic, and ritual are key ingredients in countless frameworks for medicine and health the world over, and such remedies—placed as they are within complex and robust frameworks of relationship and worldview—are not what I am referencing in this piece. The place of astrology, magic, and ritual in Western medicine is only a slight tilt away from the more accepted but precarious places of herbalism and energetic approaches. The precarity and lack of robust context within which astrology operates in the West opens it up to co-optation and abuse. The optimization mutation that turns external productivity into internal renovation merges with the endless opportunity of astrological play-by-plays to create a perfect storm of frustration and failure that continues to feed itself.

Rather than a technology of narrative and orientation offering broader meaning and connection, astrology under optimisation culture easily becomes another gamified process to track and maximize. We obsessively develop and refine techniques and protocols, often in the absence of more narrativizing and orienting rituals such as Hersey's "naps" or Han's "festivities." Every action becomes technologically timed and controlled, sometimes to the second, waiting for the best astro-weather and avoiding the worst, typically fashioned more according to externally acquired technical rules rather than more intuited or divined relational guidance. Every action, purchase, creation enacted at the chosen time becomes an investment intended to pay off in the future, the pay off a key aspect of self-optimization. The "belabored self" of Micki McGee's *Self-Help Inc.: Makeover Culture in America* takes on not only the role of the one working but also the one being worked upon.[8] The same criticisms that can be leveraged toward modern self-help, diet, and therapeutic cultures can be leveraged toward self-optimization, as well.[9] Encouraging productivity, efficiency, and the logics of capital, as technologies of self-fashioning and self-management, self-optimization practices go beyond crafting ideal citizens and workers, and toward crafting ideal consumers.

To be clear, I love and practice electional astrology and transit-tracking. I am Virgo enough to relish an optimizing mindest from time-to-time, but I witness the insidious possibilities of such practices when their main operating context is the digital late stage capitalism pressure vortex with purity culture, eugenics, and rising fascism buttressing the edges. The Borg from *Star Trek*, with their collectivist privileging of efficiency above all else, were the ultimate villains of 90s American television for similar reasons, but what is striking and prophetic about them for the 21st century is their appetite for consumption and novelty, constantly desiring new knowledge, technology, and ideas only to ruthlessly flatten it all into their own joyless sameness, their own optimized perfection.

This is the violence of whiteness: any aberration that cannot be consumed and nullified—that cannot be *optimized*—is the enemy. Many astrologers who came into the ancient revival tributaries of astrology due to their rising popularity of the last decade found relief in language and cosmology that is inclusive of experiences of harm, oppression, trauma, and violence. But when practiced within the vortex described above, the language of malefics, bad houses, detriment, and fall are often misunderstood and weaponized, most often against oneself. Without a broader spiritual and magical, even religious, context that offers agency and understands the chart as so much *more than* simply a diagram of an atomized individual life potential, the pressure to self-optimize can swoop in.

The major point of pause in electional-type transit-tracking for self-optimization comes when instead of focusing outwards on *action* and *participation*, our practice focuses on *feeling* and *wellbeing*. As someone who lives with chronic health struggles and experiences of disability myself, and who serves many folks as an astrologer who is known to be supportive of those with similar lived experiences, I believe that living attuned to the cycles of the planets, diurnal circling of the houses, and heliacal motions of the stars is a gorgeous way to connect to being alive. But I also hold focus on a collective lens regarding celestial attunement, which in turn maintains the participatory element integral to cultivation of relationship.

An experience of a Venus retrograde period, for instance, is always properly a collective experience, no matter what is being activated in a natal chart. A transit can certainly be more immediate and embodied when the natal chart and timing techniques indicate its importance, but the insistence that every lunation and passing aspect must be experienced *personally*—and can thus be personally optimized—is a fallacy of hyperdigitalization and disconnection. The fleeting natures of feeling and wellbeing are more adequately attended to through local land and spirit practices, including ancestral connectedness. Cultivating relationship with the celestial spheres through craft, through devotional, theurgic, magical, or ritual engagement, makes their living cycles personal in a way that watching (ourselves watch) an elaborate clock incessantly tick simply can not. If astrology is going to be hijacked by optimization culture, it can simultaneously Trojan Horse magic, dreams, and spirit back into any materialism that attempts to co-opt it.

No matter how, where, or when one's astrology is rooted, the posture of much contemporary astrology is anticipation. The next lunation, the next transit, the next profection, the next planetary return, the next Great Conjunction. There is a throwing forward and displacement of one's anxiety, desire, fears, hopes, and dreams, and unlike the generalized nature of those affects shared by many, those with astrological literacy are given objects in the form of temporalities to attach to in anticipation.

In the story of Pandora in Hesiod's *Works and Days*, all the evils of the world are released—toil, sickness, disease, pains—except ἐλπίς, Elpis, most commonly translated as "hope," meaning expectation or anticipation accompanied by a level of certainty.[10] Especially in a post-Obama context where the word "hope" itself has been evacuated of its meaning, the ongoing millennia-long debate over the exact meaning of Hesiod's exception is far beyond our purview here. But the landscape of astrology offers a site of practice for whether this posture of anticipation is a good—which true certainty has been kept from many prognosticating humans—or an evil—whose certainty we remain protected from.

In the hyperconsumerist society where we make a living, astrologers are often responsible for creating anticipation and anxiety through our specialized and technologized information, and then offering solutions—ideally through narrative, orientation, and meaning, but also through more techniques for optimizing one's role as consumer. Commerce is as sacred as astrology to Mercury, and there are more and less ethical ways to go about all this, surely. Each of us must decide for ourselves the values we embody in our astrology.

The values we hold closest in our astrology have far-ranging consequences. On May 6th 2019, while Jupiter was retrograde in Sagittarius, the United Nations-convened Intergovernmental Science-Policy Platform on Biodiversity and Ecosystem Services released their *Global Assessment Report* on rates of species extinction and threats to life on Earth.[11] The report draws the dire conclusion that the Earth's biodiversity has undergone "unprecedented" change in the last fifty years, irrecoverable loss of quality and quantity of wildlife and habitat, and over a million species are now threatened with extinction. In the report's recommendations for policy-makers, the IPBES lists a number of mutually reinforcing "levers" for intervention that can create lasting change toward sustainability "where efforts yield exceptionally large effects." The number one intervention offered by the *Global Assessment Report* is "visions of a good life," suggesting "enabling visions of a good quality of life that do not entail ever-increasing material consumption" where second is "total consumption and waste."[12] The priority of prevention, from the more familiar reduce/reuse/recycle pyramid, is incompatible with the values of hyperconsumerism, and thus the culture shift of visions is also a necessary intervention. We can see this intervention in various subcultures purporting slowness and simplicity, although many of these movements can play into the traps of white supremacy and neo-colonialism in their nostalgia for a past that comes with social and cultural inequalities that have since been tended, or at least recognized.

There is no going back—as astrologers have been technology nerds forever—but there is a possibility of deepening and amplifying the values supportive of life, connection, and celestial-terrestrial connection. To many current practitioners of astrology who adopt a relational, magical, animistic, embodied approach, the debate between Fate and Free Will is over. To be re-placed within a cosmology that recognizes the linkages between the celestial and terrestrial hierarchies of spirits and substances, into which we—as expressions and creations of the divine—are intertwined on the material and spiritual is to make an intervention into the perfect storm of frustration and failure.

Byung-Chal Han writes, "The mania for health and optimization is a reflexive response to the lack of being…Because being is *being-with*, isolation and loneliness lead to a lack of being…The lack of being causes an excess of production…We *produce against* the feeling of lack…A feeling of lack impels us to act."[13] In the world of the belabored self, that act is often consumption and often under conditions of urgency and scarcity, the next attempt to discover the one best way. Astrology is positioned to offer interventions into this cycle of lack, optimization, frustration, loneliness, and consumption as a practice of orientation and narrative, of possibility and dreams, of making new visions of a good life. Challenging defaults of urgency and scarcity is tricky in a discipline defined by the uniqueness of moments in time, but reconciling our practices with the need for spaciousness and generosity is medicine for the birthing of these new visions.

As we approach the Jupiter opposition of the *Global Assessment Report* while Jupiter moves through Gemini next year, these questions could be tough to keep asking, so I want to leave you with one now:

What does a slow astrology look like?

I find my own answers in the spirals and dance of relationships—human and more-than human, planetary and stellar, dirt and sky, daemonic and chthonic, somatic and intellectual, technical and intuitive, story and experience, text and quest, presence and absence, local and global, future and past, now and then, now and when. I find my own answers of spaciousness and generosity among my fellow astrologers. The majority of us—even with differences and disagreements—*love* this craft of astrology with an ardent flame of devotion and inexhaustible well of reverence, and I love that about us.

Notes

All URLs last accessed in May 2024.
1. Byung-Chul Han, *Vita Contemplativa: In Praise of Inactivity*, Trans. Daniel Steuer, (Polity, 2024).
2. Michael Sacasas, "The One Best Way Is a Trap," *The Convivial Society.* Substack, 2023. https://open.substack.com/pub/theconvivialsociety/p/the-one-best-way
3. Tricia Hersey, *Rest is Resistance: A Manifesto,* (Little, Brown Spark, 2022).
4. Ibid.
5. Daniel Nehring and Anja Röcke, "Self-optimisation: Conceptual, discursive and historical perspectives," *Current Sociology*, OnlineFirst, 2023. https://doi.org/10.1177/00113921221146575
6. Ibid., 1.
7. Ibid., 6.
8. Micki McGee, *Self-Help Inc. Makeover Culture in America* (Oxford UP, 2005), 16.
9. Nehring and Röcke, "Self-Optimisation," 13.
10. https://www.theoi.com/Heroine/Pandora.html
11. IPBES (2019): Summary for policymakers of the global assessment report on biodiversity and ecosystem services of the Intergovernmental Science-Policy Platform on Biodiversity and Ecosystem Services. S. Díaz, J. Settele, E. S. Brondízio, et al. (eds.). IPBES secretariat, Bonn, Germany. https://doi.org/10.5281/zenodo.3553579
12. Ibid., 17.
13. *Vita Contemplativa.*

GIACOMO ALBANO

"Earthly Stars":
The Cycles of the Stars
in Natal Astrology

In the previous article we examined the role of the extreme declinations of the stars in world astrology. This article explores how the fixed stars and their extreme declinations play a very important role in a natal chart.

First, check whether the natal planets are parallel or antiparallel to the minimum or maximum declination reached by some important stars. By "important" I do not mean the brightest stars, but above all the more important stars in the natal chart, e.g., due to their angular position, aspects with the planets, heliacal phases, parans, parallels and contraparallels (based on their current, not extreme declinations).

Therefore it is necessary that 1) declination parallels exist between the natal planets and the extreme declinations of some stars, and 2) these same stars must also play some role in the natal chart based on their current position (by whatever type of aspect, phase, parallel, paranatellonta, or angular position). The presence of these two conditions can lead to important and particular manifestations of these stars in the native's life and represents one of the "secret" reasons why the apparent similarity of two natal charts can lead to two people experiencing vastly different events.

This also happens because the stars' extreme declination is linked to their "initiatory" potential, or at least to the most remarkable and special effects they will produce during the precessional cycle.

Limit- stars and Sirius, the "Southern Pillar" in Giza

Let us first conceive the power of the *limit-stars*, giving an example of the Limit-Stars in Giza to precede our analysis of Johann Bach's nativity to follow. The Egyptians conceived the cardinal points as Pillars connecting the Earth with the Sky. When examining the stars which touch the horizon in the cardinal directions, we can examine the *limit-stars* of a certain earthly latitude (which culminate and anticulminate on the North and South points of the horizon), or we can examine the *equatorial stars* which will always rise and set in the true East and West points, valid for all latitudes.

Every latitude thus has its *limit-stars*, and their particular strength lies in the fact that they touch the horizon when they are very close to—or coincide with—the cardinal point North (if they are northern stars), or South (if they are southern stars). These stars have a declination equal to or opposite to the colatitude of the place. A colatitude is the complementary angle of a given latitude, i.e., the difference between a right angle (90°) and the latitude. For stars at the same value of the colatitude, they will be circumpolar and visibly grazing the horizon upon their anticulmination, and conversely, they will be anticircumpolar invisible, grazing the horizon on their culmination.

We can also observe when the star's limit is in the heliacal rising altitude: the rising star crosses the local horizon and reaches its visible heliacal rising altitude while it is also close to North or South, i.e., very close to the meridian, which naturally runs North to South. This is especially true for fainter stars, whose light appears only when they are one or more degrees above the horizon.

Sirius reached its minimum declination of -60° beneath the equator and so became the limit-star at +30° latitude, since we defined the limit stars with a declination equalling the complement of the latitude, and adding to 90°. As fate would have it, +30° latitude is exactly that of Giza, the place where the Great Pyramid was built. In my book *Ancient Egypt, Jerusalem and the Stars* I defined Sirius as the "Southern Pillar" at Giza because at its lower precessional stopping point at -60° South of the equator, the star could only touch the horizon when it culminated, i.e., when it reached its maximum altitude (=0°) during its diurnal motion. This means that Sirius could only touch the horizon when it was exactly South (culmination at 0° altitude). See Figure 1, facing page.

The stopping point coincided with a cardinal direction, and the star thus "consecrated" the local horizon, with effects felt throughout its cycle, that is, until the star will reach its next minimum declination. This is the power of the limit stars of a certain latitude, during a certain precessional epoch. North of Giza, Sirius became completely anti-circumpolar and thus completely invisible during the years of its minimum declination. Of all the reasons why the Great Pyramid was built at Giza, this is certainly the most convincing, and strongly

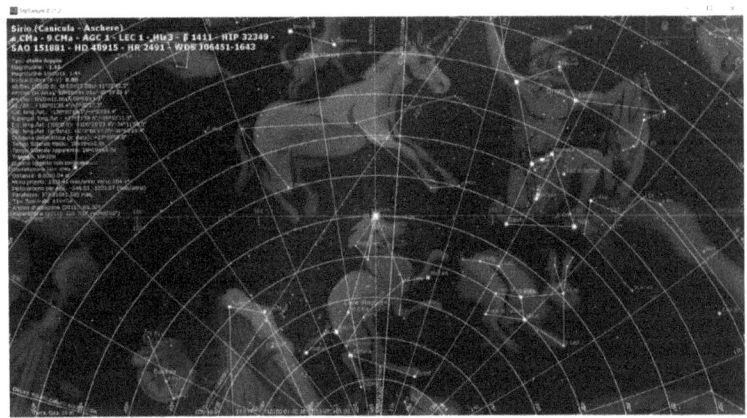

Figure 1: Culmination of Sirius in Giza at its precessed minimum declination (lower stopping point): the star could only touch the horizon when it also touched the meridian, arriving exactly South.

suggests that the Egyptians knew and used the technique based on the extreme declinations of the stars.

Johann Sebastian Bach, Fomalhaut and the constellation Columba

The stars that most favor musical talent have the nature of Venus or Venus-Mercury. The stars belonging to the constellations of songbirds (especially Columba, but also Cygnus) or musical instruments (Lyra) are the most specific.

When Johann Sebastian Bach was born, Venus and Mercury were conjoined and Venus-Mercury-Jupiter were parallel at the maximum declination of Fomalhaut (just over +6°). Fomalhaut (*Alpha Piscis Austrini*) has a Venus-Mercury nature and highly favors talents in the arts and sciences. It is also one of the four "royal" stars.

Venus-Mercury-Jupiter-Fomalhaut: it was precisely the similar nature of the planets and the stars that had such a strong effect. Perhaps the Moon itself was also conjunct Fomalhaut (as we do not know the time of birth, we cannot say for sure).

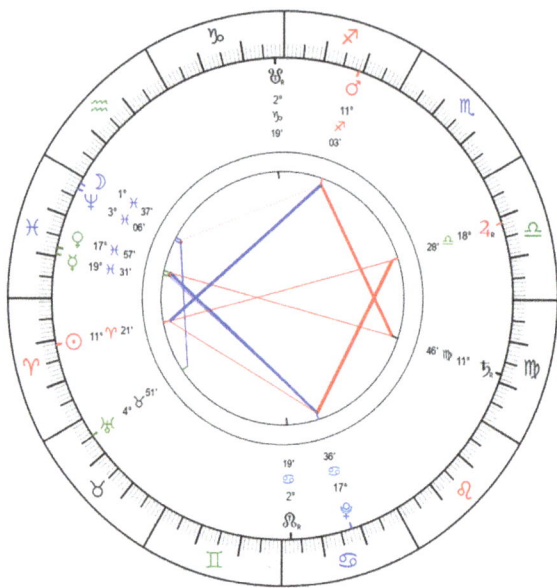

Figure 2: Chart of the planets on J. S. Bach's birthday. RR: X.

But there is more. On the day of Bach's birth, the Venus-Mercury conjunction was in paran with Wazn (*beta Columba*): the conjunction was setting while the star was rising (and it too has a Venus-Mercury nature). Wazn was also in paran with the Sun: the setting of the Sun took place while the star was culminating. We would not be surprised if some of these stars were angular when he was born, but unfortunately we do not know the time of birth (See Fig. 2, above).

Wazn (beta Columbae), Eisenach's Limit-star

According to Ptolemy, the heliacal rising of stars can take place when they reach a height above the horizon that corresponds to their apparent magnitude. In the case of the third magnitude stars, this is about 3° ("I metodi moderni dell'Archeoastronomia" di Adriano Gaspani e Silvia Cernuti).

Wazn (*beta Columba*) is a third magnitude star that was at maximum declination in Bach's time. At the latitude of the composer's hometown (Eisenach), the star could reach its heliacal rising altitude only in the period of its maximum declination. Until then it was too low on the horizon, even when it reached its culmination altitude.

From an astrological point of view, that this very important phase of Wazn's cycle took place precisely in the years of its maximum declination, is *very* significant. In the following centuries, as the declination decreases, Wazn will be anti-circumpolar again and will no longer be visible from Eisenach. And this applies not only to Wazn, but to most of the stars in the constellation: *delta, kappa,* and *epsilon* Columba were also limit-stars at Eisenach.

In other words: in Bach's hometown, many Columba stars began to rise heliacally only in the period of their maximum declination, i.e., in one of the two phases of their 26,000 year cycle in which they have their maximum strength and in which they reach their "stopping point," greatly magnifying the power of the star, in addition to the parallels and parans which also link it strongly to his birth.

The first heliacal rising of these Columba stars in Eisenach thus signaled their important earthly manifestation in this place through the birth of an *"earthly star"* of music, and perhaps the greatest musician of all time. I like to define "earthly stars" as all those things and beings that are an evident and luminous manifestation of one or more stars in our earthly dimension. Among these "earthly stars" there are certainly also illustrious people.

Declination Families and "Antidote-stars"

Two stars that have a minimum or maximum declination which is also parallel or contraparallel to each other are connected, and over the centuries, the mixture of their natures and meanings will be recognizable in many important events. For example, say in 11,000 BCE a star precessed to a maximum at +20° declination, and then in 600 BCE, another star precessed to a minimum at -20° declination. These two stars are now connected for the entire precessional cycle, and any point that crosses this declination (either by parallel or contraparallel) is tied into it. Any two stars connected in this way form "declination families," which are simultaneously triggered at the same declination, even when the stars are no longer there.

In most of these "declination families" there are both benefic and malefic stars. And one of the possible effects of this combination may be that the former have the power to neutralize or mitigate the evils of the latter. In the medical field, this also refers to the concept of "antidote-stars," which is one of the topics of my book *Medical Stellar*

Astrology. The idea is that the benefic stars that are part of a "declination family" can become potential "healers" against the ills caused by the malefic stars having the same extreme declination or the opposite (contraparallel). In the natal charts of great physicians, some of these "families" are activated in a particularly significant way that ensures the predominance of the benefic stars.

The astrological factors we find in the natal charts of great physicians are also of great interest to the researcher for another reason, namely that if we know these factors, we can identify the best "antidote-stars," which have the power to neutralize or alleviate the evils caused by some malefic stars. This is of particular interest in medical electional astrology and astrological magic.

The Contra-antiscion Alhena/Rasalhague and its Therapeutic Virtues in Alexander Fleming's Natal Chart

Alexander Fleming was a Scottish physician and microbiologist who is best known for discovering the world's first effective antibiotic substance, which he named penicillin. Alhena is a benefic star of Venus-Mercury nature in the feet of Gemini. It was parallel to his natal Sun. Fleming was born on the day of the heliacal rising of Alhena, and the star was rising and freshly visible just at the time of his birth. (See Fig. 3, facing page.) The declination of Alhena was still very close to its recent maximum, making the star more powerful than other stars belonging to the same "declination family."

Alhena's declination of +16°30′ was equal to the minimum of Rasalhague (*alpha Ophiuchi*), a malefic star belonging to the same "declination family." Rasalhague is the main star of Ophiuchus, another constellation associated specifically with diseases. Given that a benefic star can act as an "antidote" to the evils caused by the other stars, Fleming was in an ideal position to manifest the antidote-powers that Alhena had towards Rasalhague.

Here we come to one of the most interesting and significant points of our analysis. The Moon (20° Sagittarius) was exactly conjunct Rasalhague (20° Sagittarius), and its contra-antiscion was conjunct Alhena (7°27′ Cancer). At that time, the contra-antiscion Alhena-Rasalhague had an orb of about 2°. The orb tightened and the antiscion became practically perfect by the precession of the tropical cross in the year of the discovery of penicillin (1928). But it only perfected to the minute of arc in 1941, the year penicillin was

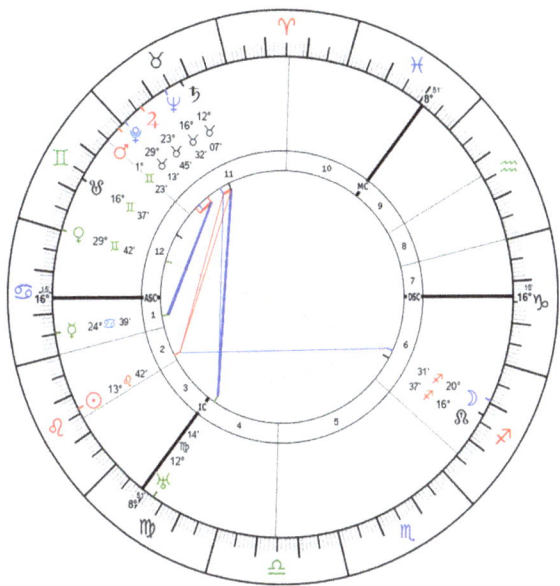

Figure 3: Alexander Fleming. RR: AA.

first used against bacterial infections! In my books I discuss the importance of antiscia and contra-antiscia between two stars, which perfects for small periods of time as the tropical zodiac creates new antiscial alignments to the projected degrees of stars by precession. Antiscia are another type of relationship between two stars that can also be used in medical electional astrology, namely when we are looking for an "antidote-star."

Antiscia between stars always brings important events, and their effect is even stronger when the two stars are already linked through their extreme declinations, as was the case with Alhena and Rasalhague. So in Fleming's time, the relationship between Alhena and Rasalhague was back in force. Fleming's natal chart (through the Moon, but not only) intercepted these potentials at the highest level and gave the benefic Alhena a clear preponderance, as the star was rising heliacally at the time of birth.

This is a form of Hermetic astrology, and one of its most fascinating aspects is that the most salient features of a natal chart are hidden from modern view, and they turn out to be nothing less than the powerful activation and manifestation of stellar potentials.

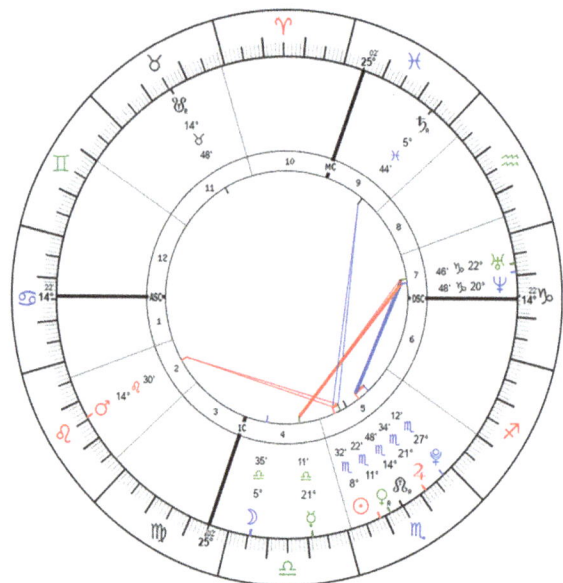

Figure 4: Amazon's website launch. RR: AA.

The Secrets of Amazon Website

The day the Amazon website was launched (Figure 4, above), the Sun's declination was equally parallel to the minimum declination of Castor (-14°50′), a bright and benefic star with the nature of Mercury. On that day there was a Sun-Castor paran to boost the connection, and as the Sun set, Castor anticulminated.

The declination of the Sun (-14°) was also equal to the minimum of Zubeneshamali (*beta Librae*), a benefic star of Jupiter-Mercury nature, and the much luckier and higher scale of the two. That same day, Jupiter and Zubeneshamali were also in paran; they both had the same right ascension and so culminated at the same time. This "equatorial" conjunction was perfect to the minute of arc! Moreover, there was the heliacal setting of Jupiter and Zubeneshamali, so both were very powerful by their annual heliacal phase. Therefore the Sun was connected to Zubeneshamali both by the parallel to the star's minimum declination and by the heliacal phase, and Jupiter was connected by an equatorial conjunction (co-culminating paran) and

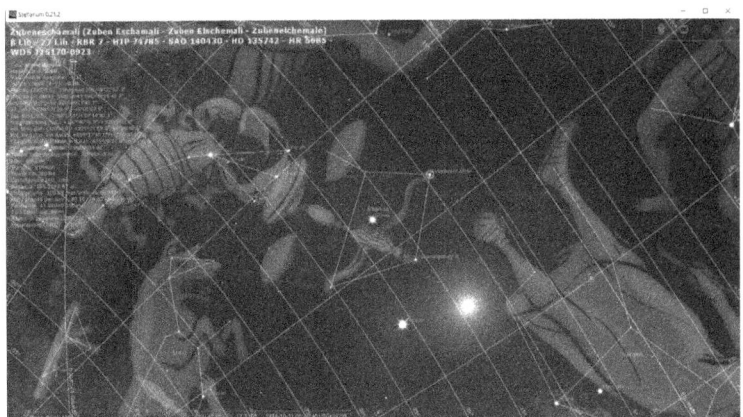

Figure 5: Jupiter was in the constellation of Libra and had exactly the same right ascension of Zubeneshamali (an equatorial conjunction), so the planet and the star culminated at the same time that day.

entering the same heliacal phase on the day of the website's launch. See Figure 5, above.

Castor and Zubeneshamali belonged to the same declination "family," though not perfectly (minimum between -14° and -15°). Recall that a great effect is achieved when a natal planet is both parallel to the extreme declination of a star and in other zodiacal aspects to that star. The Amazon website chart activates the long-term connection between Castor and Zubeneshamali because the Sun and Jupiter are in aspects and parallels to both stars simultaneously. And the Sun and Jupiter were also connected to each other by Jupiter's heliacal phase, and through the parans with mutual stars.

Much of Amazon's extraordinary fortune is precisely due to the strong activation of this long-term connection between two benefic and business-friendly stars. The Sun and Jupiter support these positive effects in great magnitude, and anchor these stellar factors into the nativity of the website with powerful force.

Conclusion to the Stellar Techniques for Nativities

Some of the secrets of the extraordinary fortunes of some natal or event charts lie in the simultaneous activation (by the right planets) of two or more stars belonging to the same "declination family." Of course, the nature and strength of the activating planets also plays a role. If the activating planets had been different or in worse condition, the effects would also have been different.

We are only scratching the surface of these methods. More analysis, examples, and methods can be found in my books. In any case, our discussion of nativities and "Earthly Stars" here grounds us into the importance of the seven planetary spheres as the anchors for stellar consciousness from the firmament into the earthly spheres.

Chart Data

In order of appearance:
JOHANN SEBASTIAN BACH, 21 Mar. 1685, n.t., Eisenach, Germany. Source: https://www.astro.com/astro-databank/Bach,_Johann_Sebastian
ALEXANDER FLEMING, 6 Aug. 1881, 2:00am GMT, Darvel, Scottland. Source: https://www.astro.com/astro-databank/Fleming,_Alexander
AMAZON WEBSITE, 31 Oct. 1994, 9:00pm PST, Reno, NV. Source: https://www.astro.com/astro-databank/Business:_Amazon_Website

MATT TREASE

from In the Belly: an Imbolc daysong

9:33 AM

Today is Imbolc in the Gregorian rhythm, that beat of Roman time, slightly slower than the empire beat, that totalitarian edict that devoured sun and moon to create a uniformity we are still under the spell of—*Quantity*. We measure days with gears and years with tables. Before Caesar, time was counted an interrelation of the lunar cycle and the solar cycle, so that time was made by the relationships of earth to moon to sun to the fixed stars. Since the 1st century, we've slowly been forgetting the role of the moon with its slightly asynchronous beat with the sun, its rhythm that gives us our sense of a day, a sense of relativity and time, how it all unfolds with slight variations, improvisations—

>enough of a gap for us to fill
>
>to escape the perfect
>
>circularity of fate

10:06 AM

In order to become pervaded with, and an incorporation of the spirit, one must begin to work with that in which spirit manifests. One must begin to think and feel in terms of relatedness and of individualized wholeness. One must deal, astrologically speaking, with cycles of relationship rather than with cycles of positions.
                                                         Rudhyar knew
the universe is not a clock, though it does lend its prototype. Time is about relationships that recur within the cosmos, about patterns that connect. In this standard

rhythm, today is a quantified halfway point between the winter solstice and the spring equinox. I am trying to tie together those turnings of the wheel, of the year, to flesh out time from death to rebirth.

In Ireland, The Mound of the Hostages, a Neolithic tomb passage, was oriented so as to allow the dawn light in only two days a year—Imbolc and Samhain—those quarter points in the dark night of Proserpine's time in the underworld—a reminder that the dead are never dead, only sleeping, awaiting that rhythmic orphic calling to awaken to begin anew,

        a new form, a new

        shape, a new channel

        for living, like the rain

culled to heaven from bodies below, falling in this open field to reemerge in the grass, the weeds, the Doug Fir, lending shade to the stargazers lying dormant in this earth.

Note: this excerpt is from a poem composed spontaneously during the course of a single day, February 1, 2024.

ROBERT P. BLASCHKE

On Progression Theory

The systems of birthchart progression are derived from the natural celestial measurements of time: our Earth revolves daily on its polar axis while the Moon appears to orbit monthly around the Earth and, simultaneously, both the Earth and Moon orbit yearly around the Sun. This raises a fundamental theoretical question in astrology: What are the relationships between a day, a month, and a year?

This interrelationship between the different celestial movements is the foundation for the systems of horoscope progression. Secondary progressions—day for a year—reflect the movement of the planets one day for each year of life. Tertiary progressions—day for a month—reflect the movement of the planets one day for each lunar month of life. Minor progressions—month for a year—are the movement of the planets one lunar month for each year of life.

Table 1 - Progressed Planetary Movement

Progression	Actual Movement	Symbolic Time
Secondary	one day	one year of life
Tertiary	one day	one lunar month of life
Minor	one lunar month	one year of life

If the secondaries are calculated as one day of planetary movement per year of life, then what are the relative rates of speed of the tertiaries and minors? Tertiary progressions, which move the planets one day for each lunar month, would then produce ± 13.37 days of planetary movement per year. Minor progressions, which move the planets one lunar month for each year, would then produce ± 27.32 days of planetary movement per year. Thus, an approximate time ratio of 1:13:27 exists between secondary, tertiary and minor progressions. It is my belief that this ratio defines how time operates at three different rates of speed, and how its three-dimensional qualities can be perceived through the three different progression calculation techniques.

Progressions have been likened to the hands of a clock, with the slow-moving secondaries as the hour hand, the medium-speed tertiaries as the minute hand, and the fast-moving minors as the second hand. Alan Leo, in *The Progressed Horoscope*, written almost a hundred years ago, outlined a similar analogy using secondaries, minors and the diurnal chart.

Progression Theory—Metaphysical

No doubt the metaphysician in you has experienced pure intellectual joy in your studies and practice of astrology. One particularly sweet spiritual experience results from reflection on the planetary glyphs and their deeper meanings. Common in the literature on esoteric and theosophical astrology are references to the circle of Spirit, the crescent of Soul, and the cross of Matter. Also mentioned are the physical, emotional, and mental bodies that envelop the spiritual self. These three symbols—circle, crescent, and cross—are variously found in each of the planetary glyphs and help the student of astrology to comprehend the essence of the planetary archetypes.

Extending metaphysical correlations to progression time theory, the Sun is represented by the circle of Spirit and correlates to the year; the Moon is represented by the crescent of Soul and correlates to the month; and the Earth is represented by the cross of Matter and correlates to the day.

Table 2 - Metaphysical Correspondences I

Symbol	Spiritual Meaning	Celestial Body	Time Measure
Circle	Spirit	Sun	Year
Crescent	Soul	Moon	Month
Cross	Matter	Earth	Day

Going deeper into the mysteries of the three systems of progression, secondary progressions are the relationship between the Earth and Sun—day for a year. Tertiary progressions are the relationship between the Earth and Moon—day for a month. Minor progressions are the relationship between the Moon and Sun—month for a year.

Table 3 - Metaphysical Correspondences II

Progression	Celestial Relationship	Time Relationship
Secondary	Earth-Sun	Day-Year
Tertiary	Earth-Moon	Day-Month
Minor	Moon-Sun	Month-Year

Journeying further into this theoretical framework, secondary progressions are the relationship between Matter and Spirit (Earth-Sun), tertiary progressions are the relationship between Matter and Soul (Earth-Moon), and minor progressions are the relationship between Soul and Spirit (Moon-Sun).

Table 4 - Metaphysical Correspondences III

Progression	Celestial Relationship	Spiritual Relationship
Secondary	Earth-Sun	Matter-Spirit
Tertiary	Earth-Moon	Matter-Soul
Minor	Moon-Sun	Soul-Spirit

Emerging from the other side of the looking glass, we see that secondary progressions define the experiences of the physical body (Spirit entering Matter—Time Ratio of 1:1); tertiary progressions define the experiences of the emotional/astral body (Soul entering Matter—Time Ratio of 1:13); and minor progressions define the experiences of the mental/causal body (Spirit entering Soul—Time Ratio of 1:27). In this cubic paradigm, we find reality operating on three different levels and, simultaneously, at three different rates of speed.

Table 5 - Metaphysical Correspondences IV

Progression	Dimension	Spiritual Relationship	Time Ratio
Secondary	Physical Body	Spirit Enters Matter	1:1
Tertiary	Emotional Body	Soul Enters Matter	1:13
Minor	Mental Body	Spirit Enters Soul	1:27

Note

Excerpt from Robert P. Blaschke, *Progressions*, Astrology: A Language of Life Vol. 1, second edition (Olympia, WA: Revelore Press, 2024).

Figure 1: Takens in the military c. 1891; © Aleida Mosselman

C. Aq. Libra
Roelf Takens (1862–1930),
Esoteric Astrologer and Writer

IN THE MID 1970S, both a Dutch and an American publisher took the same 60-year-old astrology book off the shelf, reprinted it, and presented it to the public as a classic.[1] *Astrology, Its Techniques and Ethics* first appeared in 1914 in Dutch. Anyone "who seriously studies astrology will certainly want to own this book," the Dutch publisher lured the potential reader in 1976 into buying it, for although at times it was "a bit old-fashioned and moralizing," its essence was "inimitable."[2] The American publisher praised it as "amazingly clear and inspirational," "an important occult work...to those interested in the role of the stars in man's spiritual evolution."[3] The author was Roelf Takens, who used the pen-name C. Aq. Libra.[4] According to the Dutch publisher, Takens had been an astrologer, a writer, a veterinarian who specialized in horses, and an amateur painter. Supposedly, he had worked in a town in the north of the Netherlands, and at some point, settled in The Hague. In the meantime, he had travelled to Cairo, North America, and Lugano. No more information was available. So, by the end of the twentieth century *Astrology, Its Techniques and Ethics* was a classic, but had mostly lost the connection to its author—and with that its roots in time and place.

In 2012, I discovered a copy of the book, the Dutch, second edition printed in 1916, together with two others written by the author—*Cosmos en microcosmos* (1915) and *Symbolen en mythen in religie* (1922)—among the esoteric book collection of an aunt when I emptied out her apartment after her passing. This collection consisted of a few hundred varied volumes, mainly obtained between 1910 and the early 1960s, and was part of the legacy of my aunt's husband and his parents, who all had passed long before her. My relatives held no importance in any esoteric movements. They were just individuals living a mundane life in The Hague. The very same is valid, to a degree, of Roelf Takens. In the grand scheme of esoteric teachings, he is not an outstanding individual. He is only remembered as the author of *Astrology, Its Techniques and Ethics*. Nevertheless, my motive to write about him is precisely to shed light on an obscure figure who has become part of an "in between" layer in society, a man who grasped various teachings of well-known esoteric figures and who transmitted his knowledge to individuals, such as my uncle's parents. In addition, I will argue that Takens' activities as an artist may have sparked his interest in Theosophy, and that his former profession as a vet contributed to his disquisition of esoteric astrology, which led *Astrology, Its Techniques and Ethics* to become a classic within astrological discourse.

Takens' Whereabouts and Works

Roelf Takens was born at 11:00 p.m in the evening on October 2, 1862, in Winsum, a town in the north of the Netherlands (53N20, 6E31) which, like similar towns and villages in the province of Groningen, organized an annual event of harness racing.[5] For both Takens' parents, the marriage was their second. He was child number four of

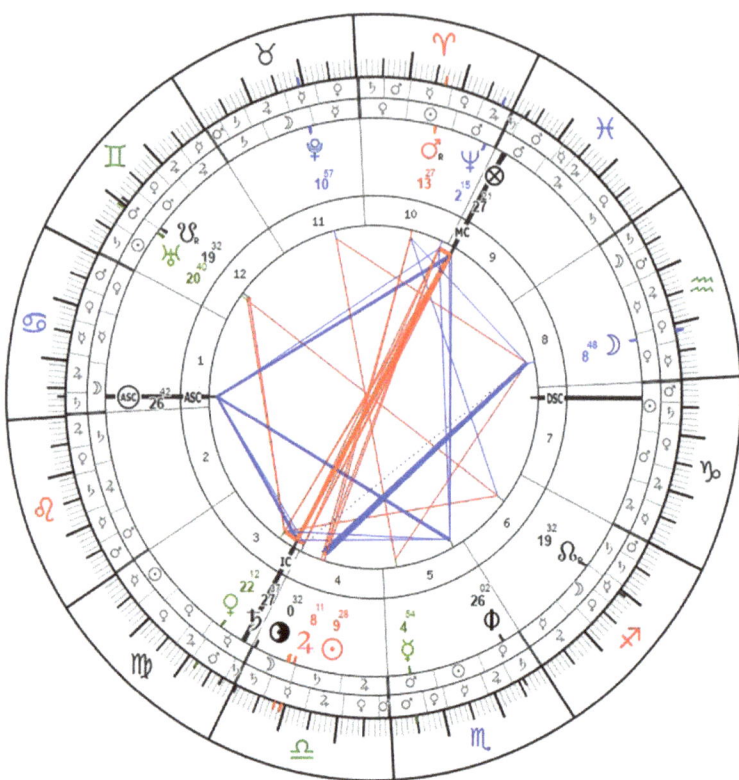

Figure 2: Roelf Takens. Source: Astrodatabank; RR: AA.

the five this Dutch Reformed pair conceived, and he was the only one to survive.[6] Roelf's mother was an innkeeper (Dutch: *logementhouder*, *herbergierster*), who had inherited the business from her first husband; his father was a carpenter and contractor who, due to the second marriage, became an innkeeper as well.

At the age of eighteen Takens was admitted to the veterinary school in Utrecht. He obtained his diploma in July 1886, and soon after found employment as an inspector of the newly built livestock market and abattoir in Amsterdam.[7] Then, in the spring of 1890, he was appointed state horse veterinarian of the army in the Dutch East Indies. The contract lasted for five years, after which the military granted him a yearly pension of 600 guilders. Contrary to expectations, Takens spent only two years of this commitment in the East. Troubled by eye problems, he was allowed to return to his home country and enroll in a new course of study. By October 1894, Takens had passed all the exams at the University of Utrecht to become a dentist. In that professional capacity, he held practice, first in Hoorn, a town near Amsterdam, then in the city of Groningen. Once a week he either devoted some hours to treating the poor for free at his practice, or he spent a full day in a surrounding village to see patients unable to make the trip to the city to consult him.

Still, Takens must have longed to be back in the archipelago of the Far East. At the end of 1898, or in the beginning of 1899, he boarded a ship, and for more than a year travelled and worked, as a dentist, in the Dutch East Indies. By March 1900 he had returned to Groningen. From April to July, he operated a dental practice in Amsterdam, only to take off again in the summer of 1901 to spend another full year in Java and presumably other islands of the Dutch colony in the Far East.

Somewhere along this line, or after his return to the Netherlands in 1902, Takens began to paint and engrave. For a brief while he joined the art society St. Lucas in Amsterdam: they showed some of his works during their exhibition of May–June 1908. Prior to this, galleries in Leiden, Rotterdam, and Cologne had displayed some of Takens' paintings, watercolors, pastels, and etchings. Except for a handful, all these works are now lost.[8]

Between 1908 and 1909, Takens was known as a retired horse vet travelling to Cairo. In May 1909, after the passing of his mother, he went to the United States and spent a year in Los Angeles.[9] In June 1912 he began a year-long world tour, which took him to Genova, Port Said, Cairo, Jerusalem, Batavia, Singapore, Hongkong, Japan, Hawaii, Mexico, Los Angeles, Grand Rapids (Michigan), and via London back to Italy, where he intended to stay for a while.[10] During the month of March 1916, Takens was at Lago Maggiore. By August 1918, when coming from Lugano, Switzerland, he settled anew in The Hague, this time married to Louise Fanny Margaretha Geldmacher (Papiermühle, 1876–after March 1941). Still more travels followed: London and Hastings (UK) in 1921, Rheinburg (Gailingen, Germany) in 1922, Zurich in 1923, Locarno (to attend a conference) in March 1924, Tegna and Lago Maggiore in 1925, Calcutta, Adyar (the Theosophical Society) and Yogyakarta in 1926, and Genova in 1927. During mid-April 1930, Takens embarked on the steamship Rotterdam IV to New York. According to a genealogy website he passed away, presumably abroad, on October 21, 1930, at the age of 68.[11]

In tandem with his globe-trotting, Takens took up writing. His earliest publication appears to be an article about the painter and engraver Fernand Desmoulin (1853–1914), mostly known for his mediumistic drawings produced between 1900 and 1902. Takens had visited Desmoulin in October 1907.[12] The article came out in *Het toekomstig leven* (*The Future Life*), a semi-monthly journal published by Harmonia, the Dutch Association of Spiritualists. His next article dates to 1909. Here, Takens describes his trip on a Chinese vessel from Oleh Leh, the port at the most northern end of Sumatra, to Penang, Malaysia. It is illustrated with four of his own drawings.[13] Five years later his book, now a classic, was published.[14] Five others followed. The last of these volumes, *Innerlijke kosmologie* (*Inner Cosmology*, 1925), is the compilation of Takens' articles on astrology published in 1922 in the periodical *De Tempel* (*The Temple*).

Another series of articles appeared under the heading "Eene mystieke reis" ("A Mystical Journey").[15] These were published in 1923 in the periodical *De Nieuwe Gids* (*The New Guide*) and involve Takens' year around the world travel of 1912–1913. Takens claims to have edited the diary notes written in 1920 by a friend named Ralph van Winsen, which Takens then drafted into chapters. Since Ralph is the English counterpart of Roelf, and the family name "van Winsen" is an obvious reference to Winsum, the village where Takens was born, the articles simply stem from Takens' own memory, and, most likely, his own notes. The chapters narrate a quest: particular events having taken place during a journey (Takens' 1912–1913 world tour) are viewed from, and interpreted through, Takens' mature lens of 1920. They involve, among descriptions of the various environments and interactions with people, encounters with a spirit guide named Leophallus, and an out-of-body experience. Quite a few anecdotes are garnished with "astrological knowledge."

What remains are Takens' translation of, so he alleged, a manuscript prepared by a Caucasian named Vano Koleloff,[16] four articles in *De Tempel* that were not part of the "Inner Cosmology" series,[17] four more contributions to *De Nieuwe Gids*,[18] a letter published in the short lived astrological magazine *Lilith*,[19] three unpublished poems,[20] various letters sent to the editors of *De Nieuwe Gids*,[21] plus Takens' claim of a privately published brochure written in English.[22] Together, C. Aq. Libra's output comprises much more than anticipated on the basis of the information provided by the two publishers in 1976.

Takens' Writings in Context

Roughly divided, Takens wrote either about astrology from an all-encompassing (holistic) perspective, or from his travel experiences. The split is not always clear cut. His astrological writings are larded with anecdotes from abroad, and his later travel journalism is tinged by his interest in the occult, especially astrology.

For the modern reader, Takens' narrations and musings about his travels especially arouse a mixture of bewilderment and fascination. Vivid descriptions of people of various cultures, in all kinds of circumstances, lead to an intimate throwback in time, along with opinions that by now are highly outdated and therefore occasionally shocking.

Takens' take on astrology is rooted in the teachings of the Theosophical movement. By stating not to build on H.P. Blavatsky's *The Secret Doctrine*, he intended to fend off probable criticism towards some of his ideas that would not be in harmony with those of Blavatsky and other Theosophists.[23] He sided more with the German Theosophical milieu: *Astrologie* (1914) contains various references to Rudolf Steiner (1861–1925), who lectured in the Netherlands in 1908[24] and who parted from the Theosophical Society at the end of 1912 to become the founding father of the Anthroposophical Society. The connection with the German milieu comes even more to the fore in the German translation of Takens' first book. *Astrologie, Ihre Technik und Ethik* (1915) is supplemented by a series of brief descriptions of horoscopes of well-known people, among them Steiner,[25] *and* the book has many small illustrations, drawn by Takens, three dozen of which reference drawings created by Fidus, the pseudonym of the German symbolist artist Hugo R.K.J. Höppener (1868–1948).[26]

When and where Takens began to study astrology is unknown. Most likely he was introduced to Theosophy first, perhaps already in the Dutch East Indies, where at the turn of the century a center of the Dutch Theosophical Society blossomed in Semarang.[27] But it is also possible that he was first exposed to the teachings of François Charles Barlet, the pen-name of the French occultist Albert Faucheux (1838–1921). Takens dedicated his last book, *Innerlijke kosmologie* (*Inner Cosmology*, [1925]), to Barlet, his "highly regarded Teacher and Friend." Earlier he wrote appreciatively about Barlet, whom he had visited at his home on the Rue des Grands-Augustins in Paris. He shared that Barlet had named his two cats *Soleil en Libra* (Sun in Libra) and *Lune en Sagittaire* (Moon in Sagittarius).[28] Perhaps these names inspired Takens to pick his own pseudonym.

The former vet and dentist may have met Barlet around the time that he spoke with the above-mentioned Fernand Desmoulin, in 1907. Barlet had been an early member of the Theosophical Society in France and subsequently participated in numerous occult societies. According to Jean-Pierre Laurant, Barlet was not a magus, but someone who "aspired to make occultism into a positive science" for which end he considered astrology to be "the most suitable means."[29]

Yet it is equally possible that Takens was introduced to Theosophy in the artistic milieu he must have dwelled in for some time in the Netherlands around 1908.

Interest in astrology had increased among members of the Theosophical Society. Highly important in this regard is Alan Leo (pseudonym of Frederick W. Allen, 1860–1917). Leo became the founding father of what is called "esoteric astrology." This type of astrology focuses on the evolution of the soul and builds on the concept of the "seven rays" as presented by Blavatsky and developed further by others.[30] It sparked a major new development in the history of astrology, for Leo, and those after him, assigned a central role in the horoscope to the Sun; astrology became Sun centered.[31]

This renewed interest for astrology began around 1900, and soon reached the Netherlands. In 1903 the Theosophist, freemason, and publisher Hendricus J. (Henri) van Ginkel (1880–1954) was the first to write about Leo in Dutch.[32] Three years later van Ginkel and Leo launched the journal *Nederlandsch Tijdschrift voor Moderne Astrologie*, a Dutch periodical for "modern astrology." The following year it was renamed *Urania*. Only recently, the journal changed into a digital newsletter.

Right from the start, the former naval officer in the Dutch East Indies Adolph E. Thierens (1875–1941) was involved in *Urania*. According to Kim Farnell, Leo had met Thierens during a visit to the Netherlands in 1903.[33] This is unlikely, since Thierens himself claimed to have been introduced to astrology only in 1904, whereupon he joined the Theosophical Society.[34] Thierens' official registration at the lodge in The Hague took place in April 1906. It is more likely, therefore, that Leo met Henri van Ginkel in 1903.

The following year van Ginkel published his Dutch translation of Annie Besant's *Esoteric Christianity* (1901). During the summer of that same year, 1904, van Ginkel was initiated into freemasonry by Besant, together with six others.[35] Perhaps Thierens was among these others.

Soon after, Thierens founded the Dutch Association for Astronomy and Modern Astrology and became an astute astrologer in the Netherlands approaching the subject from the Theosophical perspective. Under the editorship of van Ginkel, Thierens and Miss J.E. Vreede,[36] *Urania* was turned into the Society's official organ. What is important to note is that this association was not exclusively devoted to Theosophical astrology. It appealed, therefore, to a broader audience than just Theosophists interested in astrology.

Roelf Takens was involved in the Dutch Society for Astronomy and Modern Astrology at least for a while during his later years, namely when living in The Hague in the 1920s. After registering in May 1920 as a member of the Theosophical Society, Takens joined *Urania*'s board of editors in 1923. Although he was a keen astrologer, Takens did not submit any articles to *Urania*. Furthermore, he did not practice astrology as a profession, that is, he did not cast other people's horoscopes, even if they were willing to pay him for such services.[37] Takens advised those interested in their own horoscope to study astrology themselves, and to struggle alone, or with a few comrades, in composing one's own natal chart. For only in this manner, he opined, he or she would discover the depth of this most interesting "science" properly.[38]

While in The Hague, Takens also became one of the many editorial board members of *De Tempel*. This bi-monthly magazine dedicated to "free religion" existed from the beginning of April 1923 until October 1927. The organization behind *De Tempel* consisted of a partnership of multiple groups and organizations with a wide range of "free religious" beliefs.[39] It befitted the Theosophical doctrine at that specific time, namely that all religions could and should be expressed, because, so the Theosophists believed, all religions would evolve and eventually lead to a single global religion led by the guidance of a new religious world master. Leading figures of the Theosophical Society assigned this messianic role to Jiddu Krishnamurti (1895–1986). Takens did not follow the latter, but he did believe that the Age of Aquarius had just begun. This new era, he calculated, would last approximately 2,160 years.[40]

The Reception of Takens' Astrology in the Netherlands

Based on the reprints and Takens' subsequent writings, it is obvious that Takens' take on astrology was well received by the public at large. Nevertheless, the handful of published reviews range from positive to quite critical. "C. Aq. Libra, hiding between what in plain Dutch could have been 'K. Wat Weegschaal' [K. What Scale] does not cast your horoscope, but offers the instructions from which you can cast your own," a journalist opined in a brief review while making fun of Takens' pen name.[41] One simply has to know the place, date and hour of birth, and with the aid of Raphael's *Astronomical Ephemeris of the Planets* is able to decipher someone's "life in the Cosmos." Obviously, the reviewer considered "esoteric astrology" too simplistic to determine an individual's character and personality.

Positive, but at various points quite critical because of sloppy details or reasoning, is the apothecary and Theosophist Anna C. Alblas-Sorber (1868–1929) in her review of Takens' astrological elaborations in *Cosmos en microcosmos* (*Cosmos and Microcosmos*, 1915). She was pleasantly surprised to find that the author's general knowledge included the field of medicine, in particular his explanation of plants corresponding to planets (Paracelsus), and his view that abstracted chemical components of plants cannot replace the healing properties of the plant as a whole.[42] Supporting this point of view, she stated that she could add to Takens' examples, namely cases she was aware of through her own work.

Alblas-Sorber's lengthy review in *Urania* was followed by an equally lengthy one of A.E. Thierens. Thierens first praised *Cosmos en microcosmos*:

> C. Aq. Libra is a born astrologer and this makes this work both entertaining and worth reading almost everywhere. It is rarely, if ever, unimportant. Astrology lives for him, and he shows throughout this book that one cannot live Astrology without loving Nature in all her realms with great interest. *Astro*-logy is after all the knowledge of the connection between heaven and earth, thus of the soul of Nature![43]

However, Thierens then takes issue with many of Takens' astrological ruminations. He also explains how Takens' claim to write from his *own* perspective and not Blavatsky's or any other Theosophist's, could not stand: Takens simply copied ideas from Steiner.

So he queried: "Why be ashamed of the *Secret Doctrine* of Mrs. Blavatsky, yet built on Dr. Steiner's?"[44]

The reviewer of *Cosmos en microcosmos* in the monthly journal of the Dutch Theosophical Society was even more critical. He complained that Takens mocked scientists in general, because they would critique Theosophy and astrology, something that, according to the reviewer, was not correct per se. Also, Takens uncritically copied sections of a variety of authors, and posited opinions without any argument to sustain them. On top of this, Takens did not cite much from Annie Besant or equally important Theosophical authors, nor did he refer to the three volumes of Thierens' cosmology, whereas these would enlighten the reader much more than Takens accomplished. The reviewer ended with just a single positive note: the book had "some really nice illustrations."[45]

Perhaps such critiques were expressed out of envy. This is, after all, the explanation Cornelis van Es (1896–1946) offered when he, a salesman and aspiring astrologer, presented C. Aq. Libra in *Lilith* as the astrological pioneer in the Netherlands. (The first pioneer presented in this periodical was Alan Leo.[46]) "Like all finer minds ahead of their time," van Es noted, C. Aq. Libra "has been vilified and his work has been broken down, mainly in his native country, by some jealous 'fellows.'"[47]

Takens himself, a modest man, living his life for a higher, "evolutionary" purpose, seems to have developed a thick skin for negative remarks. It shows in the way he responded to van Es, who had complained about unfair critiques regarding his own astrological work. Criticism is "the best publicity you can get," Takens had commented.[48] Besides, "it aren't the worst fruits the worms gnaw on," "one rarely receives a financial reward for labors of love," yet such labors "make loyal friends."[49]

The Novelty of Takens' Astrology

Through his many travels, Takens made friends worldwide. These connections may have been the motive for the Dutch publishing company P. Dz. Veen to get *Astrologie* (1914) out in both German and English. By doing so, Takens' esoteric astrology reached a larger audience than Thierens' did during the 1910s and 1920s.[50]

The subsequent interest in, and success of, *Astrologie/Astrology* can be accounted for by the comprehensiveness and humanness

Takens embedded in the new, Theosophical take on astrology. His esoteric astrology was related to history, religion, mathematics, astronomy, and medicine. Or, even more importantly, astrology seemed to be the foundation of life on Earth with all its various aspects. Part of this was a result of encounters with many cultures, but Takens' academic training and medical professions especially must have affected his understanding of esoteric astrology.

Compared to Leo and Thierens, Takens was equally proficient in cementing the celestial bodies (macrocosm) to the human body (microcosm). All three men were able to present the metaphysical and technical knowledge of the movements of the planets as something highly relevant for the private life of any individual. Yet Takens did so by addressing in much more depth issues that traditionally have always been important aspects of astrology: health and the physical body.[51] Astrology shows us the "*weak points of our* character in all their nakedness," Takens expounded, and it "teaches us how, by calculation, to find the time when these weak points in our character will be liable to manifest."[52] Knowing this, he continued, allows us to be prepared through methods such as "meditation, self-communication etc.," so we can "warn off these disturbances in our physical and spiritual health."[53]

Within the "medical" passages Takens refers to *Medical Astrology* (1908) by Heinrich Däath, *Raphael's Medical Astrology* (1910) by Raphael Patai, and *Die Diagnose aus den Augen* (*The Diagnosis from the Eyes*, 1911) by N. Leljequist, and more.[54] Obviously, he consulted those writings. Nonetheless, the flow in his writing indicates that far from merely coping the content, he genuinely understood what it was about. In other passages it comes across as if he wrote from personal experience as a vet, for instance when he discusses the "pre-natal horoscope" that, in his view, "often explains the premature death of children," and can aid "in studying deformities, arising during the intra-uterine life."[55] His experienced understanding also shows when he reasons that astrologers can help doctors, especially "where it concerns internal affections that are hard to diagnose," and "various acute diseases" of which it is known that "a crisis comes after a number of certain days."[56]

According to Takens, many physicians in the United States, England, and France were including astrology in their practices and were thriving "as well as their patients."[57] He did not offer any names, though, and I have no clue as to whom he might have in mind. Takens knew at least one influential psychologist, pharmacist, and Theosophist personally: the French man Émile Coué (1857–1926). At some point, Coué had invited Takens to learn about his method of autosuggestion and healing by assisting Coué at his clinic in Nancy. Takens had accepted the offer, and during the time of his stay, he was, so he wrote, witness to a multitude of "miracle" healings.[58] Yet as far as I know, Coué did not incorporate astrology in his healing practice.

Last but not least, at least for the Dutch audience, a few illustrations Takens incorporated in *Cosmos en microcosmos* added to the novelty of his take on astrology. In particular, two of his paintings carry some religious, Christian resemblances but the titles bring them in sync with esoteric astrology. Takens "esoteric" art did not contribute to *Astrologie/Astrology* becoming a classic, but it may be an angle for further investigations once his whole body of work is taken into account.

Final Words

Whether Takens used astrology in his own practice as a dentist seems unlikely. He retired at a young age, and around 1907 was known as a retired horse-vet, not a dentist. Except for *Astrologie/Astrology* being considered a classic and relatively recently printed in Danish and Bulgarian, I have only seen it referred to as a source of inspiration to the German astrologer Elsbeth Ebertin (1880–1944) and as an early source of influence in the works of her son Reinhold Ebertin (1901–1988).[59] Nevertheless, as an obscure figure in the field of esotericism, Takens' holistic astrological ideas will have been a source of inspiration and wisdom to numerous "anonymous" people similar to the parents of my uncle, who owned and studied three of Takens' books.

Roelf Takens Publications

Koleloff, Vano (C. Aq. Libra, translator [and author], foreword). "Oergrond des levens," *De Tempel* 3.14/15 (1925): 254–58, 274–77; subsequently published as *Oergrond des levens*. Amsterdam: De Vrij Religieuse Tempel, 1925.

Libra, C. Aq. (Roelf Takens). "Antwoord aan de Redactie." *Lilith* 1.8 (April 1924): 117–18.

--. *Astrologie, beknopte inleiding*. 's-Gravenhage: Luctor et Emergo, 1922.

--. *Astrologie, haar techniek en ethiek*. Amersfoort: P. Dz. Veen, 1914, 1916 (revised ed.).

--. "Cornelia Koller." *De Tempel* 2.14 (1924): 268–69.
--. *Cosmos en microcosmos: Een astrologisch-theosofische beschouwing.* Amersfoort: P. Dz. Veen, 1915.
--. "De Mercuriusstaf." *Lilith* 1.10 (1924): 149–52.
--. "Der Schatz des Lebens: Hymnen der Mandeërs." *De Tempel* 2.3 (1924): 53–54.
--. "Eene mystieke reis: Avonturen van een globetrotter." *De Nieuwe Gids* 38.1–11 (1923): [vol. 1] 1–10, 151–77, 301–32, 453–75, 667–91, 810–40; [vol. 2] 93–114, 186–210, 320–44, 516–36, 623–47; subsequently bundled into at least one copy *Eene mystieke reis: Avonturen van een globetrotter.* 's-Gravenhage: Luctor et Emergo, 1924.
--. *Innerlijke kosmologie: Een studie van het kosmische en het microkosmische zieleleven.* Amsterdam: De Vrij Religieuse Tempel, 1925.
--. "Indrukken uit Palestina." *De Nieuwe Gids* 42.7–9 (1927): 71–84, 123–37, 262–74.
--. "Lourdes." *De Tempel* 1.18 (1924): 483–84.
--. "Mijne rustkuur." *De Nieuwe Gids* 37.11 (1922): 696–703.
--. *Neptunus-gedachten.* 's-Gravenhage: Luctor et Emergo, 1921.
--. "Ochtendwandelingen op den Montparnasse." *De Nieuwe Gids* 39.8 (1924): 186–202.
--. "Over de leer der perioden." *De Tempel* 3.14 (1925): 214–16.
--. "Over de polariteit in land en volk." *De Nieuwe Gids* 41.1/2 (1926): 72–96, 162–174.
--. *Symbolen en mythen in religie: Geïllustreerde uitgave met portret van den schrijver.* 's-Gravenhage: Luctor et Emergo, 1922.
Takens, R. "Bezoek aan het teekenmedium Desmoulin." *Het Toekomstig Leven* 11.24 (1907): 389–90.
--. "Met de Hok-Kanton van Oleh-Leh naar Pinang." *Elseviers Geïllustreerd Maandschrift* 19.37 (1909): 170–74.

Notes

This paper was presented at the International Theosophical History conference in Naarden, the Netherlands, on October 7, 2022.
1. The companies Ankh-Hermes in Deventer, the Netherlands, and Borgo Press in San Bernardino (Newcastle Publishing), California, reissued respectively *Astrologie, haar techniek en ethiek* (1914, revised by the author in 1916, 1923, and revised in 1956 by J.C. van Wageningen) and its English translation *Astrology, Its Technics and Ethics* (1917). The Dutch 1976 edition had reprints in 1978, 1979, 1980, 1986, and 1995 (all by Ankh-Hermes). The English edition, in 1917 translated from Dutch by Jacoba R.G. (Coba) Goedhart (1899–1949), had reprints in 1980 (San Bernardino Press), 2009 (Goldstein Press), 2010 (Kessinger Publishing, and Nabu Press), 2014 (Literary Licensing), 2015 (Forgotten Books, and Andesite Press), 2018 (Franklin

Classics), and 2021 (Alpha Editions).
2. The Dutch publisher's information about Takens is printed on the book's cover, and copied on various internet sites, for example https://www.goodreads.com/book/show/11811506-astrologie, consulted on February 14, 2024.
3. See the back cover of *Astrology, Its Techniques & Ethics* (1976).
4. Takens' pseudonym outlines his horoscope, which has the "Sun in Libra, Moon in Aquarius, and Cancer rising (…): C(ancer)-Aq(uarius)-Libra" (Cherry Gilchrist with assistance from Rod Thorn & the Saros Roots Group, "The Dutch Astrologers and the Soho Cabbalists," *The Soho Cabbalists*, http://www.soho-tree.com/blog/the-dutch-astrologers-and-the-soho-cabbalists, last modified on February 15, 2021).
5. P. Noord, "Harddraverij met paarden in Winsum," *Infobulletin Winshem* 5.1 (2000): 10–12.
6. Takens' parents were Jan P. Takens (1824–1890) and Rikkerdina J. Fokkens (1824–1909). Both had one surviving child of the previous marriage. Since Roelf Takens' siblings and his half-brother died young, he only had one half-sister, see note 9.
7. "De wordingsgeschiedenis en groei van het Amsterdamsche abattoir en de veemarkt," *De Vee-en Vleeschhandel* 11.98 (1927): 23–25.
8. The Rijksmuseum in Amsterdam obtained two of Takens' engravings via the collector François G. Waller (1867–1934) (F.G. Waller, (W.R. Juynboll, ed.), *Biographisch woordenboek van Noord-Nederlandsche graveurs*, ['s-Gravenhage: Martinus Nijhoff, 1938], 321). I traced on the internet no more than six images of Takens' paintings, and two small etchings.
9. Takens' travel to the US must have involved a visit to his half-sister Jacoba Hekma-Albertsma (1854–1938). She had immigrated to Grand Rapids, MI, in 1884, together with her husband and their children (cf. "Jacob Hekma †," *Nieuwsblad van het Noorden*, February 23, 1949; Libra, *Astrologie*, 265 [1914 ed.]; Idem., *Eene mystieke reis*, 536).
10. To finance the travel, Takens had (part of?) his own art collection—paintings and watercolors of the Hague School—auctioned on November 12, 1912 ("Op de veiling," *Het Nieuws van den Dag*, November 6, 1912).
11. Aleida Mosselman-Takens, https://www.genealogieonline.nl/en/genealogie-roelf-pieters-takens/I486.php (consulted September 30, 2022; personal email exchange on September 15 and 21, 2014). Takens' widow returned to The Hague at the beginning of August 1931. She then arrived from Hannover and left at the end of September for Osnabrück.
12. Takens, "Bezoek." The widower Desmoulin had married in 1905 the widowed Emma H.E. Loder, née van Oosterom (1869–1957). Emma van Oosterom was the daughter of a sugar planter in Madioen, Java. She had lived in The Hague after the passing of her first husband, a brave military man in the Dutch East Indies ("H.A. Loder †," *Algemeen Handelsblad*, March 25, 1900). Most likely Takens had known, and perhaps befriended Emma's first husband, and through her had acquainted Fernand Desmoulin.

13. Takens, "Met de Hok-Kanton."
14. Soon after, the publisher took care of bringing a German (1915) and English (1917) translation onto the market. Over a decade later the book was translated into Danish as *Lærebog i astrologie* (1930, 1970), reissued in 2020 as *Astrologiens Teknik og etik*. The first half of the book, probably the German translation, was translated into Bulgarian (perhaps by Petar Manev, who lived in Vienna from 1924 to 1928, but which was only published first in 2019, see https://slovoto.info/астрология-нейните-техники-и-етик/, last modified July 19, 2019). Another section of the work was translated into Malay by Tan Gin Ho (1880–1941), a Chinese bureaucrat, and published in Cirebon, a port city in northern West Java, under the title *Wet dari karma dan Wet dari reincarnatie* (*The Law of Karma and the Law of Reincarnation*, 1938) (Ku Wei-ying & Koen De Ridder (eds.), *Authentic Chinese Christianity: Preludes to its Developments*, [Leuven: Leuven University Press, 2001], 180–81; cf. Wikipedia, *Tan Gin Ho*, https://en.wikipedia.org/wiki/Tan_Gin_Ho, last modified November 3, 2021).
15. At least one series of these articles was bound together as a book in which the pages maintained the original page numbering. The book was not marketed. This—presumably single—copy was digitalized in 2022 by the Royal Library, The Hague, see https://www.delpher.nl/nl/boeken/view?coll=boeken&identifier=MMKB31:041550000 (consulted February 14, 2024).
16. Since I have not been able to find traces of someone named Vano Koleloff, and the mood and style of the narrative resembles Takens' other writings, it is most likely that Takens created the story about this "wise man," whom he claimed to have encountered in 1916 in the surroundings of Lago Maggiore. Perhaps Koleloff is modeled after the poet, translator, and for a while follower of Steiner, Lev Lvovich (Leo) Kobylinski (Moscow, 1879 – Locarno, 1947). Kobylinski settled in Switzerland in 1911 and he was in a relationship with Johanna H. Polman Mooij, née van der Meulen (1874–1959). She was one of the initial board members of the Dutch Society for Astronomy and Modern Astrology. Therefore, it is likely Takens knew the couple (Heide Willich, *Lev L. Kobylinksij-Éllis: Vom Symbolismus zur ars sacra*, [München: Verlag Otto Sagner, 1996], 180).
17. Libra's article entitled "Lourdes" is about a visit to Lourdes; "Der Schatz des Lebens" ("The Treasure of Life") narrates about a volume of twenty poems written by the German physician Hermann Haase (-); "Cornelia Koller" is about the Swiss trance medium/writer Cornelia Koller (c. 1880–after 1924), author of *Vorwärts* (1912), and in "Over de leer der perioden," Takens writes about *Zur Periodenlehre* (1925) by the German physician and biologist Wilhelm Fliess (1858–1928).
18. Libra, "Mijne rustkuur" ("My Rest Cure"), is a story about Takens' "friend" Ralph van Winsen; it precedes the "mystical journey" series (see note 15). The text "Ochtendwandelingen op den Montparnasse" involves a stroll on the Parisian cemetery Montparnasse. "Over de polariteit in land en

volk" ("On the Polarity in Land and People," 1926, divided in two parts) and "Indrukken uit Palaestina" ("Impressions of Palestine," 1927, cut into three parts) are written as letters to a friend.

19. Libra, "Antwoord" ("Answer"), and "De Mercuriusstaf" ("The Staff of Hermes"). The latter is an elaboration on Hermann Haase's article on that subject published in *Lotus-Blätter* (cf. the reference to Haase in note 17).
20. The poems are entitled "Prayer," "Involutie" ("Involution"), and "Reis" ("Journey") and dated c. 1922 (archive no. 69F37, Royal Library, The Hague).
21. Four of Takens' letters to the editor of *De Nieuwe Gids*, Willem J.T. Kloos (1859–1938), are kept in the Literature Museum in The Hague, as are two letters to the archivist Willem Moll (1888–1962). Twenty-six other letters to *De Nieuwe Gids*, dated 1922–1927, are kept in the Royal Library in The Hague. Willem Kloos was a founding member of the Dutch literary Movement of Eighty that initiated *De Nieuwe Gids*.
22. According to Takens' own words, he wrote the brochure *The Meaning of Life and Evolution* (1913) in Los Angeles and distributed the five-hundred copies printed among those interested in his ideas. In this brochure, so he claimed, he prophesized the outbreak of World War One (Libra, *Eene mystieke reis*, 331, 522).
23. Libra, *Cosmos en microcosmos*, 8.
24. Steiner's first lecture, "De Initiation des Rosenkreutzers," took place on March 5, 1908 in The Hague, the second, "Theosophie, Goethe und Hegel" on March 8, 1908 in Amsterdam.
25. The other horoscopes concern the Theosophists Helena P. Blavatsky (1831–1891), Henry S. Olcott (1832–1907), and Annie Besant (1847–1933); emperor Wilhelm II (1859–1941); the politicians F. August Bebel (1840–1913), Otto von Bismarck (1815–1896), William E. Gladstone (1809–1898), and Abraham Lincoln (1809–1865), and the well-known men Johann W. von Goethe (1749–1832), Vincent van Gogh (1853–1890), Martin Luther (1483–1546), and Alfred R. Wallace (1823–1913). Takens probably copied some of the sample horoscopes from Alan Leo's *Esoteric Astrology* (1913), which also contains those of Annie Besant, Otto von Bismarck, and W.E. Gladstone.
26. Libra, *Astrologie, Ihre Technik und Ethik* (1915; reprints in 1919, 1922). Also Takens' second book was translated into German: *Kosmos und Mikrokosmos* (1918) (cf. "C. Aqu. Libra", *Grazer Tagblatt*, July 28, 1920). According to the six excerpts of reviews copied on an advertisement page in *Astrologie* (1916), the German edition was well received (cf. G.W., "Astrologie," *Zentralblatt für Okkultismus* 9.4 (1915): 191).
27. Ruud Jansen, '...*een kern van broederschap*...': *100 jaar Theosofische Vereniging in Nederland* (Amsterdam: Theosofische Vereniging in Nederland, 1997), 90.
28. Libra, *Eene mystieke reis*, 342–44. Cf. Ibid., 519.
29. Jean-Pierre Laurant, "Barlet, François-Charles (ps. of Albert Faucheux)," in: Wouter Hanegraaff (ed.), *Dictionary of Gnosis & Western Esotericism*

(Leiden: Brill, 2005), 162–63. Prior, Barlet had passed on his astrological knowledge to the apothecary Abel Thomas, author of *Traité d'astrologie judiciaire* (1895) (Kocku von Stuckrad, *Geschichte der Astrologie: Von den Anfängen bis zur Gegenwart* [München: C.H. Beck, 2007], 311).

30. According to Theosophy, so Takens explained, man is a composite of body, mind, and soul, which in itself consists of seven main principles. Instead of using Blavatsky's Sanskrit names for these principles, he preferred Steiner's: the physical body, ether body, astral body, ego or "I" (Takens: *verstandsziel*; Steiner: Kama-manar or Manar), spirit self (Takens: *geestzelf*; Steiner: Monas), life spirit (Takens: *levensgeest*; Steiner: Buddhi), and spirit man (Takens: *geestmensch*; Steiner: Atma) (Libra, *Cosmos en microcosmos*, 52–61; cf. von Stuckrad, *Geschichte der Astrologie*, 319).

31. Kim Farnell, *Modern Astrologers: The Lives of Alan & Bessie Leo*, ([London]: private publication, 2019), 123–24, 201, 247–48; Falcon Kyle, "Leo, Alan (1860–1917)", in: William E. Burns (ed.), *Astrology Through History: Interpreting the Stars from Ancient Mesopotamia to the Present* (Santa Barbara: ABC-CLIO, 2018), 200–1.

32. H. van Ginkel, "Iets over astrologische invloeden," *Theosophia* 11.12 (1903): 760–78; Idem., "Hedendaagsche astrologie," *Theosophia* 12.9 (1904): 541–55. In 1905 two of Leo's booklets were translated into Dutch by Clara Streubel (1870–after 1927), and published by the Dutch Theosophical Publishing Company that was run by Johannes F. Duwaer (1869–1944) and his companion van Ginkel: *Astrologie voor iedereen* (*Astrology for Everyone*, March 1905) and *Vier lezingen over astrologie* (*Four Lectures on Astrology*, May 1905).

33. Farnell, *Modern Astrologers*, 138.

34. J.C. van Wageningen, "Pioniers der Astrologie III: A.E. Thierens," *Lilith* 1.10 (1924): 152–54.

35. Anon., *Wie was H.J. van Ginkel?*, https://gemengde-vrijmetselarij.3-5-7.nl/2016/08/30/wie-was-h-j-van-ginkel/, last modified August 30, 2016; Jansen, '… *een kern van broederschap…*', 170–72.

36. Jacoba E. Vreede (1879–1943), daughter of Theosophical parents, had studied mathematics, astronomy, and philosophy at the University of Leiden. In 1910 she became a staff member of Rudolf Steiner in Berlin.

37. Libra, *Astrologie*, [1916; Voorwoord, iv]; cf. Libra, "Antwoord," 117; l'Inconnu, "Djokjasche Causerieën XXI," *De Indische Courant*, June 29, 1926. Takens was not the only astrologer encouraging people to cast their own horoscope: already by 1910 Alan Leo did the same (Farnell, *Modern Astrologers*, 202).

38. Aided by several other astrology books than Takens', this is exactly what my uncle's father had done. With painstakingly precision, he charted in 1942/1943 the horoscopes of himself, his wife, their son (my uncle), and just two others. These charts, together with many notes were kept in the apartment of my late aunt. Among the other books on astrology in my aunt's possession were *Cosmologie: elementen der practische astrol-*

ogie (*Cosmology: Elements of Practical Astrology*, 1911) by A.E. Thierens; *Astrologie handboek* (*The Message of the Stars*, 1924) and *Astro-diagnose* (*Astro-Diagnosis*, 1932) by Max Heindel (pseudonym of Carl L. von Grasshoff, 1865–1919), and Augusta Foss Heindel (1865–1949), both translated from English; *Psychologische astrologie* (*Psychological Astrology*, [1935]) by Theo J.J. Ram (1884–1961); *Handboek der practische astrologie* (*Handbook for Practical Astrology*, 1941) by Maurice Privat (1889–1949), which was translated from French; *Inleiding tot de Wet van Cosmische Harmonie* (*Introduction to the Law of Cosmic Harmony*) anonymously published c. 1941 by the Wereld Dienst (World Service) in Ede, Gelderland, and *Astro-technica* (*Astro-Technics*, 1943) by Casper Diegenbach (1889–1962). Missing in this series of more-or-less-Dutch astrological standard works of the early 1940s are *Wat is een horoskoop en hoe trekt men dien?* (1905, 1920, the Dutch translation of *The Horoscope and How to Read It*) by Alan Leo, and any other of Leo's books; Thierens' *Cosmologie: de astrologie als levensleer* (*Cosmology: Astrology as a Philosophy of Life*, 1912), and *Cosmologie: wetenschappelijke opstellen* (*Cosmology: Scientific Essays*, 1913); *Astrologie en haar practische toepassing* (*Astrology and Its Practical Application*, 1925) by Elisabeth A.G. (Else) Parker (1877–1963), *De astrologie, haar beteekenis en draagwijdte* (*Astrology and its Meaning and Scope*, 1928) by Johannes C. van Wageningen (1895–1964), and *Astrologie, eenvoudige handleiding voor het berekenen der primaire directies* (*Astrology, Simple Guide to Calculating Primary Directions*, 1932) by J.C. van Wageningen & Wilhelmus B. Vreugdenhil (1903–1977). A.E. Thierens, Th.J.J. Ram, J.C. van Wageningen, Else Parker, and not yet mentioned Leendert (Leo) Knegt (1882–1957) belong to the group of influential astrologers in the Netherlands. Similar to Roelf Takens, very little is known about their personal lives (cf. Lloyd Haft, *Dutch Astrology—Who was A.E. Thierens?*, http://lhaftblog.blogspot.com/2020/06/dutch-astrology-who-was-ae-thierens_10.html, last modified June 10, 2020).

39. Alexandra Nagel, "The Association of Jewish Theosophists in the Netherlands: The Efforts of Louis Vet and Others to Revive Judaism," *Correspondences* 7.2 (2019): 411–39, here 428, 430–31.
40. Libra, *Astrologie*, 21 [1914], 23 [1916], 22 [1979, 7th ed.]; Idem., *Cosmos en microcosmos*, 71–72. Cf. Farnell, *Modern Astrologers*, 164, 192.
41. Book review in *Algemeen Handelsblad*, February 28, 1914.
42. A.C. Alblas-Sorber, "Boekbespreking: *Cosmos en microcosmos*," *Urania* 10.1 (1916): 30–37, here 36.
43. A.E. Thierens, "[Boekbespreking: *Cosmos en microcosmos*]," *Urania* 10.1 (1916): 37–42, here 37–38.
44. Ibid., 42. Perhaps it was under the influence of F.-C. Barlet that Takens tried to distance himself from Blavatsky.
45. D.A., "Boekbeoordeeling," *Theosophia* 23.11 (1916): 434–37, here 437.
46. J.C. van Wageningen, "Pioniers der Astrologie I: Alan Leo," *Lilith* 1.7 (1924): 101–2.

47. C. van Es, "Pioniers der Astrologie II: C. Aq. Libra," *Lilith* 1.8 (1924): 118–19.
48. Libra, "Antwoord," 117.
49. Ibid. Cf. Takens' letter to Willem Kloos, "Beklaag u niets," s.a. (Literature Museum, The Hague).
50. English translations of Thierens' astrological writings came out a decade later: *Natural Philosophy: Being an Introduction to Astrology and Occultism in General Along the Lines of Modern Scientific Thought* (1928), *Elements of Esoteric Astrology* (1931, reissued in 2013), *Astrology in Mesopotamian Culture* (1935, reissued in 2020), and *The General Book of the Tarot: Containing the Astrological Key to the Tarot-System* ([1949], reissued 2008, 2018) (cf. Haft, *Dutch Astrologers*).
51. Mark Harrison, "From Medical Astrology to Medical Astronomy: Sol-luna and Planetary Theories of Disease in British Medicine, c. 1700–1850," *The British Journal for the History of Science* 33.1 (2000): 25–48.
52. Libra, *Astrology* [1917], 13, italics in the original.
53. Ibid.
54. Ibid., 139, 198, 201, 206, 211, 218.
55. Ibid., 170.
56. Ibid., 210; Libra, *Astrologie* [1916], 294.
57. Ibid., 14, 206.
58. Libra, "Lourdes," 484; cf. Idem., *Eene mystieke reis*, 530, and "Indrukken uit Palaestina," 272. It is unknown when Takens' stay with Coué took place. However, since Coué opened the doors of his clinic in Nancy in 1910, and Takens mentioned his stay there in 1924 as if it had been some years ago, it will have been somewhere between 1910 and 1920.
59. The Astrology Podcast [with Chris Brennan and guest Jenn Zahrt], "Elsbeth Ebertin and the Rise of Women in Astrology," December 18, 2017 (https://theastrologypodcast.com/transcripts/ep-137-transcript-elsbeth-ebertin-and-the-rise-of-women-in-astrology/, consulted October 29, 2022); Florian Achthaler [bookseller Bouquinist in Munich], "Beschreibung" [by Reinhold Ebertin, *Geburtszeit und Lebensereignis* (1971)].

PETER O'LEARY

from Onlikenesses

From the author: This book-length project is called *Onlikenesses*. It stems from the Old English word for simile, which is "onlicnes." The poem consists of twelve sections of twelve stanzas each twelve lines long. The selection I've included for you come from the fifth section, which is organized around notions of interiority and psychology.

::

Like the stone drawn from the tonsil of the Sun.
Like the doom of the empty tomb that becomes
 the world.
Like all the laborious groaning, its torpid raptures,
 its pities effects.
Like all the mansions of heaven visible in one
 sweeping glance, a circulation of the song of
 creation.
Like an umbered nemesis you can see in the
 House of Death—the flow of unfortunate
 warmth from its porch.
Like the bright day sent up, torched.
Like ritual time's timorous clasp, this great
 unlevered loosening.
Like the loss of communion, unmoored
 dissipations in a world untethered from its
 altars.
Like this priestless day's stab of sameness.
Like the baritone expressions of doom.
Like giving up the ghost, one person at a time.
Like the vast outreach of an Easter felt in its
 enclosure.

::

Like Force prying open the jaws of a lion.
Like dogs swallowing the falling petals of the
 Moon.
Like monasteries enclosing a wilderness of
 holiness in their walls.
Like a chiliastic acceleration.
Like an alchemical yliaster whose vital spiritual
 power combines matter and the stars.
Like doctors, barbers, bathkeepers, students,
 servants, girls and boys, all those whose hope
 salvation consumes.
Like Paracelsus's great peregrination through
 Europe in his capacity as a field surgeon.
Like the art that is engraved in us, the art of the
 material body, of the ethereal body, and of the
 luminous body.
Like the shoemaker, the stonecutter, the scholar,
 the unawakened, those absorbed in sleep, the
 masters of the alphabet.
Like when evening extends to the end of days, its
 pilgrimages, bridges, images, river, trees.
Like a *chickadee's wince, its critical theodicies, silent
 light's agonized wash.*
Like the origin in the spirit of everything invented:
 earth, the sea, the air, the firmament,
 casualties

::

Like chiromancy, physiognomics, *substantia*, and
    customs and usages.
Like nature the sculptor.
Like the one who wields and holds human souls.
Like *my voice's thundering organ of storming
    summons, its absorption into the night's
    always-vanishing naught.*
Like the chicory who stands under the special
    influence of the Sun.
Like prophecy and art that are taught.
Like the outward forms of things, analogies.
Like the Sun drowning in the fountain of Mercury.
Like calcination, solution, separation of the
    elements, conjunction, putrefaction,
    coagulation, feeding, sublimation,
    fermentation, exaltation, augmentation, and
    projection.
Like a theory of correspondence the presence of
    pre-existing ideas in nature realizes.
Like arts full of a prophetic or sibylline spirit.
Like dreams' sidereal knowledge and geomancies'
    lies.
Like Joseph discovering in his sleep the nature of
    Mary.

::

Like doctors of theology calling magic witchcraft.
Like a magus astride the land and sea, argenteous spheres beneath his feet, a face of wind held in his left hand aloft gusting furiously, a tremoring cymbal held in his right hand aloft flaring with flukes of light, the crescent Moon and noontide Sun shining down in his crumbling world.
Like a thing completely losing and forfeiting its shape only to become something whose virtue and potency take new shape out of nothing a sorcerer seizes on in vision.
Like an alchemical tincture, a philosopher's stone.
Like sulfur's autonomous volition.
Like an arcanum, the entire virtue of a thing, different in locusts, different in leaves, different in flowers, different in ripe and unripe fruits.
Like the tincture's transformative tinges.
Like the celestial fire on Earth, a cold, rigid, and frozen fire—the body of gold.
Like the thestral kestrel's chiromantic killying.
Like crestfallen characterizations, the world's riddled film.
Like an uroboral symbol of eternity.
Like stars of folly and stars of wisdom.

::

Like reason, wisdom, ruse, strife, weapons
    dwelling in the stars just as in men.
Like paying greater heed to the words of Christ
    than to those of astrology.
Like carrying within the whole firmament and
    thus all of its influences.
Like scientists and theologians, the prophet, the
    astronomer, the apostle, and the physician as
    well.
Like the sidereal and aerial body and like the
    elemental and material body as well.
Like imitating the image of God and conquering
    the stars.
Like the primal gift of free will and the law of
    Moses and the redemptive death of Christ and
    the teaching and the example of the gospel.
Like the mystery of grace without the proclivity to
    sin.
Like Pelagius's mildness, the straightforward
    ability to choose good.
Like right wingers whose sphincters pucker at the
    thought of choosing the good.
Like taking that actual fear all the way into your
    heart.
Like thinking astrology is an actual problem.

::

ABOUT THE CAELI INSTITUTE

A library with a presence on real land

CAELI SITS ON THE ORIGINAL HOMELANDS of the Coast Salish people, at the instersection of the Nisqually and Cowlitz Tribes, within the area specified by the Treaty of Medicine Creek (1854). When land wasn't ceded through good faith efforts, it was often stolen from our Indigenous relatives. *She-nah-nam* has been home to these people for thousands of years and we honor and respect their continued presence. It is important to understand the longstanding history that has brought us all to reside on this land and to seek to understand our place within that history, even as we make it our work to understand the future.

The Celestial Arts Education Library is a member-supported research institute like no other. Our collection centers astrology in its myriad forms and the expression of celestial arts from all human cultures throughout history. We aim to right the wrongs perpetrated by scientific positivism and colonial capitalism's abuse of our craft.

Inside our walls you can research materials and artifacts found together in this way nowhere else. We are a collection of collections, and we preserve the tomes written by our ancestors, so you can build upon their works and push our field even further.

Beyond our walls, CAELi is a vibrant community united by our shared passion for cosmological inquiry. Whether you are fascinated by ancient astronomy, modern astro magic, or envisioning a celestial art of the future, CAELi is your homebase. Your HQ.

We encourage and foster deep exploration and discussion of cosmological topics, through research into the primary and secondary sources found in our physical library, as well as experimental classes in our virtual campus. We support publication of your work in various venues, such as books, magazines, or journals, such as this one!

Join CAELi today and join the fight to restore astrology's rightful place in the pantheon of legitimized knowledges. At CAELi you can push the boundaries of the celestial arts, elevate your insights to new heights, and contribute to a broader understanding of the rich field we call astrology. Are you in?

www.caeli.institute

www.ingramcontent.com/pod-product-compliance
Lightning Source LLC
Chambersburg PA
CBHW040252090526
44586CB00041B/2813